Staying Close

A Lent Course exploring intimacy with God

Staying Close

A Lent Course exploring intimacy with God

Russell Herbert

kevin mayhew

www.kevinmayhew.com

kevin mayhew

First published in Great Britain in 2015 by Kevin Mayhew Ltd
Buxhall, Stowmarket, Suffolk IP14 3BW
Tel: +44 (0) 1449 737978 Fax: +44 (0) 1449 737834
E-mail: info@kevinmayhew.com

www.kevinmayhew.com

© Copyright 2015 Russell Herbert

The right of Russell Herbert to be identified as the author of this work has been asserted by him in accordance with the Copyright, Designs and Patents Act 1988.

The publishers wish to thank all those who have given their permission to reproduce copyright material in this publication.

Every effort has been made to trace the owners of copyright material and we hope that no copyright has been infringed. Pardon is sought and apology made if the contrary be the case, and a correction will be made in any reprint of this book.

All rights reserved. No part of this publication may be reproduced, stored in a retrieval system, or transmitted, in any form or by any means, electronic, mechanical, photocopying, recording, or otherwise, without the prior written permission of the publisher.

Unless stated otherwise, Scripture quotations are taken from *The New Revised Standard Version Bible: Anglicized Edition*, copyright 1989, 1995, Division of Christian Education of the National Council of the Churches of Christ in the United States of America. Used by permission. All rights reserved.

9 8 7 6 5 4 3 2 1 0

ISBN 978 1 84867 809 5
Catalogue No. 1501504

Cover design by Justin Minns
© Image used under licence from Shutterstock Inc.
Edited by Virginia Rounding
Typeset by Angela Selfe

Printed and bound in Great Britain

Contents

About the author	6
Before you start, read this . . .	7
Introduction	9

First week of Lent
Discipleship: the call to stay close — 15

Second week of Lent
Staying close to God in the wilderness — 23

Third week of Lent
Staying close when we're feeling worried — 31

Fourth week of Lent
Staying close to the glory of God — 39

Fifth week of Lent
Staying close in our witness — 45

Sixth week of Lent
Staying close to the servant king — 53

Easter
Staying close to the risen Jesus — 61

Postscript – something for the journey — 69

About the author

Revd Dr Russell Herbert is a Methodist Superintendent minister, with a background in both youth work and theological research. He currently serves on the team at Christchurch, Clevedon, a vibrant and fast-growing ecumenical church in North Somerset.

He is also the author of *Growing through the Church: A practical and theological vision for all-age worship* (Kevin Mayhew, 2013) and *Living Hope: A practical theology of hope for the dying* (Kevin Mayhew, 2014).

Before you start, read this...

This course has been written for small groups to use during Lent. It could actually be used any time of year, but it has been structured over six sessions in order to run through the six weeks of Lent, with a seventh session for Easter.

The material is targeted towards individuals, but individuals meeting with others in a group setting. This means that it would in theory be possible to simply read this book on your own, although the discussion-based activities would need to be used as personal reflection, which is of course more limiting. It is therefore recommended that the sessions be used in a small group context. This might involve anything up to about ten participants, although a smaller group makes for a more intimate level of interaction between members. Some of the activities and action points encourage group participants to reflect or undertake a task individually. At such points, it is assumed that group members will feel comfortable and relaxed about openly sharing their thoughts. However, groups should not feel bound by this and may prefer to simply pause for quiet reflection if that is considered more appropriate.

Participants will probably find that the sessions run most effectively if a leader is appointed within the group. In recognition of the business of life, the sessions have been written so that it is just about possible for the leader to be able to lead the group with relatively little preparation beyond reading through the material beforehand. However, for groups to get the most out of each session it is recommended that all participants prepare by reading through the session's introduction, Bible passage and short commentary. This isn't essential, but it is likely to enrich the group discussion enormously.

In preparing the material, the intention has been to provide a resource that can be used more or less 'off the shelf'. It isn't intended to be regarded as a 'script' to be slavishly followed, so please feel free to adapt it in order to make it work for you.

Introduction

'God is closer to you than your own breath.' I'm not sure exactly where that quotation comes from, but it's something I have heard stated on more than one occasion. It's quite a thought. We cannot see, hear or physically touch God, but he is much, much closer to us than we recognise.

How close to God do you feel right now?

For millions of people throughout history and in the world today, intimacy with God has been and is a genuinely personal experience. God may not be visible, audible or tangible, but countless people of all ages and from vastly diverse cultures worldwide will testify to a very real sense of the presence of God. Many speak of sudden, dramatically transformational encounters that have taken place quite unexpectedly and have turned lives upside down. Others are more familiar with a gradual, ongoing experience of being held and sustained by God's presence. Whether sudden or gradual, or a combination of both, this is something that deserves to be taken seriously.

It is also very important to recognise that there are times when God can seem distant, if not altogether absent. Such reality should be taken seriously and it will not suffice to offer pat clichés in response to the searching questions that arise out of such times. Sadly, such experiences often lead people to decide that God just does not exist. That may be understandable, but it can also be too simplistic a conclusion to draw. The testimony of others who describe the positive impact of their experience of God's reality is too great to simply be dismissed on the grounds that we have not had that same experience ourselves.

Sensing the distance or absence of God is actually a very well-trodden path in the history of Christian experience. We will explore this in the second session, 'Staying close to God in the wilderness'. Here at the outset, though, we might note that at the heart of Christian faith is the story of Jesus on the cross, crying out loud with a sense of utter God-forsakenness. The experience of God's absence is to be found at what is arguably the most sacred moment of all.[1] God-forsakenness is, paradoxically, taken up into God's own experience. When we find ourselves in that place, we may thus find assurance that God has been there before us and can be found there by us. And of course, as Easter tells us, the story doesn't end there.

We may not always consciously 'feel' the presence of God. But we can be sustained in the conviction that God's closeness is far greater than our awareness of it. The sessions in this book invite you to explore this conviction and to press into it.

Intimacy with God in the Bible

The closeness of God is a recurring theme in the Bible. God frequently promises people that he will be with them, especially in difficult circumstances. Examples include Isaac (Genesis 26:3), Joshua (Joshua 1:5, 9), Gideon (Judges 6:12) and Paul (Acts 18:10). The psalmist asserts that 'The Lord is near to all who call on him' (Psalm 145:18). Indeed, Christian faith is founded on the person of Jesus – the one who is identified as 'Emmanuel', meaning 'God is with us' (Matthew 1:23). Matthew's Gospel concludes with Jesus' promise as he returns to his Father in heaven 'I am with you always, to the end of the age' (Matthew 28:20).

---

1. Matthew 27:46; Mark 15:34.

Of course, the word 'with' need not in itself denote an intimate presence. I might be 'with' other people on a bus or queuing in a shop, but that does not mean that I am 'close' to them in any personal way. It's important then to point out that, when the scriptures speak of the God who is 'with' us, they do so in a biblical context that describes that same God as the one whose presence is distinctively intimate. 'You hem me in, behind and before, and lay your hand upon me' says the psalmist (Psalm 139:5). With the same intimacy, Jesus invites, 'Abide in me as I abide in you' (John 15:4). It is in this respect that Paul describes the believer as a temple in which God's Spirit dwells (1 Corinthians 3:16); Christ is 'in' us, 'the hope of glory' (Colossians 1:27). By his grace, God becomes present *in* the believer, and the believer is given a renewed identity *in* Christ (Colossians 2:6-15; Ephesians 2:10). Therefore 1 John 4:13 declares that 'we abide in him and he in us, because he has given us of his Spirit'.

Intimacy and the mystery of God

It should be stressed that the notion of intimacy with God in no way undermines the equally important biblical assertion that God is mysterious. Whenever we talk about Christian faith as a personal relationship with the living God (which it is), an inherent danger is that the nature of this relationship, and indeed, the nature of God, may be misunderstood so that God is regarded casually. In a series of Lent lectures entitled 'Let God be God' back in 1990, Colin Morris warned of precisely this danger:

> The greatest challenge to faith in our time comes not from atheists denying God, but from believers diminishing him – treating him with sort of cosy familiarity

and addressing him as though he were 'our old pal upstairs'! There are Christians who would be modest enough to concede that they haven't the foggiest notion what's going on in the head of their pet budgerigar, but they are serenely confident that they know exactly what God thinks about the state of the economy, the poll tax, the Middle East crisis and nuclear power. Now, when we diminish God in this way, we devalue all his attributes so that his love is degraded into sentimentality, his power shades into benevolence, his holiness becomes prissiness.

There's a line in that very well-known hymn, 'God moves in a mysterious way, his wonders to perform' that runs, 'Behind his frowning countenance, he hides a smiling face'. Now the God that we present in our day very often hasn't any frowning countenance to hide behind, just the perpetual smile of a heavenly Cheshire cat.[2]

The concern here is not that it is wrong to say that God is personal and relational. Indeed, there is a sense in which Christians have a responsibility to debunk popular misunderstandings of God as some cold, disengaged deity who has little to do with everyday life. After all, says Morris, 'we want to confront a Godless generation by a God who is easy to believe in'.[3] But it is perilous when we do that simply by imagining God as everything we know and love about human beings, multiplied by a million:

> Now, our motive for doing that is quite honourable, but it is fundamentally mistaken. God is not a projection to infinity of the nicest person we've ever met. He comes

---
2. Colin Morris, *Let God be God* (London: Broadcasting Support services, 1990), p.2.
3. Ibid.

> to meet us out of the beyond as the Holy Other ... there is a strangeness about him that mocks all our cocksure God-talk.[4]

This important corrective is vital if we are to really appreciate the power of the claim that in Christ a personal relationship with God is genuinely possible. If God is nothing more than the projection of our own humanity, then it is difficult to talk about a relationship with him in any meaningful way at all. That is to say, a relationship can only exist between two parties that are separate and distinctive. It is precisely because God is so mysterious and 'holy other' that the suggestion that we might have a personal relationship with him is so powerful. Indeed, the mystery of God is itself indicative of his grace:

> Now why would God cloak himself in mystery at all? I suppose the simple answer is that if he did not cover himself in mystery we could not share this world with him. There is mercy in the mystery of God. We often talk about creation as though its purpose was to reveal God. In fact, you could equally argue that the purpose of creation is to hide God in order to protect us from the total impact of a reality that would destroy us. Demosthenes said, 'If you cannot bear the candle, how will you face the sun?'

> We cannot bear the candle. We live within the finest of tolerances. If our temperatures rise or fall by a mere handful of degrees, we die. Too much air pressure on us, or too little, and we implode or we explode. Too

---

4. Ibid., pp.2-3.

much noise, too much silence, and we go mad. We can only bear a tiny fraction of the totality of reality and, therefore, there is no way we could bear the intolerable reality of God. That is why God said to Moses, 'No man can look upon me face to face and live.'[5]

Only when we recognise the mysterious nature of God – the power of his 'holy otherness' – can we begin to appreciate the wonder of the grace by which he reaches out to us in Christ. God is mysterious, yet part of that mystery is that God invites us to open up to his closeness. This is an intimate presence that most of the time tends to be passed by unnoticed. God is much closer to us than we think. Let's explore that.

> For everyone who asks receives, and everyone who searches finds, and for everyone who knocks, the door will be opened.
>
> *Luke 11:10*

---

5. Ibid., pp.3-4.

First week of Lent

Discipleship: the call to stay close

Prayer
Lord, you have come to us in Jesus, entering our broken world and making yourself known to us in and through him. Thank you that your desire is for us to be drawn to you, to know you and to follow you. As this season of Lent begins, we pray for a deepening of our relationship with you, that we may know your closeness in ever greater depth and power, day by day. Amen.

Introduction
Do you think of yourself as a leader or a follower? The truth is, there's a bit of each in all of us.

There's a sense in which we all lead. We may not all hold positions of formally appointed leadership, but whether we recognise it or not, we all have influence on others around us through our words, actions and behaviour. We should not underestimate the ripples that our individual character makes, for better or for worse.

There's also a sense in which we all follow. That doesn't mean that we're all swept along mindlessly by the tide of popular opinion and culture. But we do all make our choices and decisions, great and small, based on things external to ourselves. Again, we may not be aware of what these things are, but all of us have our influences and we probably follow others more than we care to admit.

Christian faith is something far more radical and dynamic than deciding to believe God exists. It's about choosing who to follow, believing that when we see Jesus, we see God. Recognising this means more than just saying 'OK, I'll accept this is true'. To accept the claims of Jesus is the most fundamentally life-changing decision that it is possible to make. If Jesus actually is who he claimed to be, it changes everything. That is why from the very beginning, Christians have been referred to not only as 'believers in Jesus' but 'followers' or 'disciples' of Jesus.

Let's be clear. To become a 'follower' of Jesus does not mean that we set aside our thinking, relinquish our individuality and submit ourselves to a religious institution that will curb our freedom and stop us being our true selves. The opposite is true. It is when we make it our choice to get to know Jesus and allow our decisions and our lifestyle to be led by him that we discover a new dimension to life, a new freedom, and become truly human. That is why Jesus said, 'I came that they may have life, and have it abundantly' (John 10:10). Elsewhere, he said:

> 'If any want to become my followers, let them deny themselves and take up their cross and follow me. For those who want to save their life will lose it, and those who lose their life for my sake will find it. For what will it profit them if they gain the whole world but forfeit their life?'
>
> *Matthew 16:24-26*

Following Jesus today, just as it did when he was on earth, impacts the decisions we make every day of our lives. Sometimes that can mean that the choices we make are costly to ourselves. The word 'disciple' is closely linked to the word 'discipline', which means it involves effort, self-control and, indeed, self-denial. This can be hard work at times, but it is important to remember that none of this has to do with striving to 'earn' God's approval – his love for us is infinite already.

'Staying close' to this truth is vital if our faith isn't to amount to a mere list of prohibitions and religious rules – which can indeed be the very things that stop us being our true selves. At the heart of the gospel is the call to enter into a relationship with the living God. This must not be taken lightly or casually – it's a costly business. Jesus calls us to 'deny ourselves' – which means putting God, then others, before our own desires. But when our starting point is a conviction that God loves us inexhaustibly, then we find that the very thing we desire most *is* to put God and others before ourselves, not because we have to, but because we want to.

Activity

Think of as many different leaders as you can and write down their names. In the list, try to include some famous people, both living and from previous generations, and also other more locally known characters. Aim to include a mixture of characters ranging from public heroes through to brutal dictators.

Every leader is in fact a follower of some kind. That is to say, they are guided by something. Everyone has a belief system or set of values, as well as their own heroes and influential life experiences, even if they are not always readily recognised or identified.

Go through your list of leaders and try to identify the things or people that led, guided or influenced them.

In this first session we will be thinking about what it is and who it is that we follow in our daily lives.

Reading:
Matthew 4:12-23

Now when Jesus heard that John had been arrested, he withdrew to Galilee. He left Nazareth and made his home in Capernaum by the lake, in the territory of Zebulun and Naphtali, so that what had been spoken through the prophet Isaiah might be fulfilled:

> 'Land of Zebulun, land of Naphtali,
> on the road by the sea, across the Jordan,
> Galilee of the Gentiles –
> the people who sat in darkness
> have seen a great light,
> and for those who sat in the region and shadow of
> death light has dawned.'

From that time Jesus began to proclaim, 'Repent, for the kingdom of heaven has come near.'

As he walked by the Sea of Galilee, he saw two brothers, Simon, who is called Peter, and Andrew his brother, casting a net into the lake – for they were fishermen. And he said to them, 'Follow me, and I will make you fish for people.' Immediately they left their nets and followed him. As he went from there, he saw two other brothers, James son of Zebedee and his brother John, in the boat with their father Zebedee, mending their nets, and he called them. Immediately they left the boat and their father, and followed him. Jesus went throughout Galilee, teaching in their synagogues and proclaiming the good news of the kingdom and curing every disease and every sickness among the people.

Comment

Jesus never said 'go and make converts', but he did command us to go and make *disciples* (Matthew 28:19). There is something deeply practical about this distinction. To become a Christian goes deeper than a one-moment-in-time conversion experience. Matthew shows Jesus preaching a message of repentance (4:17) and the first sign of response to it that we see is the act of fishermen dropping their nets and literally *following* Jesus. What we believe is intricately caught up with what we *do* with our lives. And the image of *following* conveys the sense in which this is an ongoing journey, during which we can expect to discover new things (see what the first disciples discovered very soon – Matthew 4:23-24!) and continually grow.

Discussion

- The fishermen left their nets immediately and followed Jesus. What do you think it was about him that made them respond so quickly?
- The fishermen's nets (verse 20) and boat (verse 22) would have represented their way of life, their security, their livelihood, and everything they were familiar with. Can you think of a decision that you made whereby the 'Jesus way' meant making a considerable sacrifice? What would be your 'nets' and your 'boat'?
- What might it mean to be a 'fisher of people'? What might that mean for followers of Jesus today?
- The words 'disciple' and 'discipleship' are closely linked to the word 'discipline', which has to do with effort and hard work. In what ways is following Jesus hard work? What sort of effort is called for?

- The theologian Dietrich Bonhoeffer famously said, 'God's grace is free but not cheap.' What might this mean?

and there's more...

An old story is told about a young man who, while travelling in the Southern States, came across a slave auction. He was shocked and sickened as human beings were sold off as property. Eventually a young woman was pushed onto the platform. The young man watched as two men bid against one another, all the while laughing about what they were planning to do with her. Anger welled up inside the young man, and finally, he yelled out a bid equal to the value of his whole estate. The crowd was stunned, and the young man went to pay the auctioneer.

Turning to the slave, the young man said 'Young lady, you are free.'

She said, 'What does that mean?'

'It means I have bought you and I am setting you free. Here are your manumission papers,' he replied.

'Does that mean,' she asked, 'that I can be whatever I want to be, go where I want, and say what I want?'

'Yes.'

The girl, with tears streaming down her face, said, 'Then I will go with you. All I want to do is serve you.'

Authentic Christian discipleship involves staying close not to a sense of mere duty but to the grace of God.

Taking action

What practical 'disciplines' might we undertake in order to stay close to God? As a group, think about what things you might all agree to undertake between now and the end of Lent (e.g. daily reading, praying in a new way, fasting). You may come up with several different ideas, but it's probably most helpful if each individual chooses just one discipline to focus on (they don't have to be the same for everyone, of course).

Prayer

The following prayer is traditionally used by Methodist Christians in what they refer to as the 'Covenant Service'. It's a tradition that goes back to the founder of the Methodist movement, John Wesley. In the service, usually held early in the new year, the prayer is said as a way of expressing a commitment to personal discipleship. The words 'put me to suffering' do not mean that we ask God to make us suffer, but that we ask for God's help in whatever experience lies before us.

> I am no longer my own but yours.
> Put me to what you will,
> rank me with whom you will;
> put me to doing, put me to suffering;
> let me be employed for you or laid aside for you,
> exalted for you or brought low for you.
> Let me be full, let me be empty,
> let me have all things, let me have nothing.
> I freely and wholeheartedly yield all things
> to your pleasure and disposal.

And now, glorious and blessed God,
Father, Son and Holy Spirit,
you are mine and I am yours.
So be it.
And the covenant made on earth,
let it be ratified in heaven.
Amen.[6]

---

6. Trustees for Methodist Church Purposes, *The Methodist Service Book* (Peterborough: Methodist Publishing House, 1999), p.290.

Second week of Lent
Staying close to God in the wilderness

Prayer
Lord, in Jesus you have journeyed through the wilderness, and you know what it feels like to be in places of loneliness and danger. Thank you that you are with us throughout our whole lives, whatever we are going through. Help us to know, understand and appreciate that more, and so stay close to you in our thoughts and actions.
Amen.

Introduction
Dry, barren and lacking in life. That's the desert. It might be considered simply dull and featureless. On the other hand, there's something quite terrifying about the thought of being completely alone in a vast expanse of sheer 'nothingness'. It is a place where we could perish, either from the extreme night-time cold or under the exhausting heat of the midday sun.

The image of the wilderness is sometimes used to convey the way a person feels spiritually. Perhaps they may recall a time when they felt excited and passionate about God, but now they feel empty and dry. The inspiration, strength and motivation just don't seem to be there any more.

If that describes you in any way at all, here's some good news: you are in good company. The wilderness experience has been familiar territory to just about every Christian preacher, leader, pastor, mystic, pioneer and saint in history. It was St John of the Cross (b.1542) who coined the now famous phrase, 'dark night of the soul'. Sooner or later every Christian experiences it, and it can last for a very long time indeed. In this session we're going to think about how God may be found in and through it.

Activity

Spend some time in silence, thinking about the experience of walking through a desert. Try to imagine through each of your senses. What does it look like? What can you hear? What sort of smells might be around? Imagine the sensations of intense day-time heat or extreme night-time cold. If you were to place your bare hands and feet on the ground, what would it feel like? What sort of emotions would you feel? It may be helpful to write down one or two key words or short sentences that capture the images that come to mind.

Whether you have literally visited a desert before or not, the Bible reading below takes us to such a place, and helps us to explore what it means to stay close to God there.

Reading:
Matthew 4:1-11

Then Jesus was led up by the Spirit into the wilderness to be tempted by the devil. He fasted for forty days and forty nights, and afterwards he was famished. The tempter came and said to him, 'If you are the Son of God, command these stones to become loaves of bread.' But he answered, 'It is written,

> "One does not live by bread alone,
> but by every word that comes from the mouth of God."'

Then the devil took him to the holy city and placed him on the pinnacle of the temple, saying to him, 'If you are the Son of God, throw yourself down; for it is written,

> "He will command his angels concerning you,"
> and "On their hands they will bear you up,
> so that you will not dash your foot against a stone."'

Jesus said to him, 'Again it is written, "Do not put the Lord your God to the test."'

Again, the devil took him to a very high mountain and showed him all the kingdoms of the world and their splendour; and he said to him, 'All these I will give you, if you will fall down and worship me.' Jesus said to him, 'Away with you, Satan! for it is written,

> "Worship the Lord your God,
> and serve only him."'

Then the devil left him, and suddenly angels came and waited on him.

Comment

The 'wilderness' may be a universal Christian experience, but every Christian should also know that Jesus himself encountered it, both physically and spiritually. Hebrews 2:18 points out, 'Because he himself was tested by what he suffered, he is able to help those who are being tested.' Matthew, Mark and Luke all record that before Jesus entered the wilderness, he was baptised by John. This speaks to us powerfully of how Jesus both identifies with and stands in complete solidarity with us. He shares our humanity, right through to the point of suffering, dying and death. In our own wilderness experience, however bleak, Jesus is to be found with us and alongside us – Emmanuel.

Discussion

- In what ways do you relate to the experience of being in a spiritual 'wilderness', either now or in the past?

- Notice that Jesus was led by the Spirit into the wilderness, blessed with the words of his Father, 'This is my Son, the Beloved, with whom I am well pleased' (see Matthew 3:17, immediately preceding the above reading). How might this enable us to regard the spiritual 'wilderness' as part of the Father's plan for Jesus, and also as part of his plan for our lives?

- Matthew 4:2 tells us that Jesus fasted from food for forty days and nights. Fasting is perhaps something we have lost touch with in today's western culture, but it was widely practised in Jesus' day and has been right through Christian history. Why might we have reservations about it now? How might the discipline of fasting be misunderstood (and thus be a hindrance rather than a help to growing closer to Jesus)?

- In what ways might fasting, properly understood and practised, enable us to grow as Christians?

- Notice that the devil tries to test Jesus with 'if you are the Son of God . . .' (verses 3 and 6), appealing to the very words of affirmation that were given by the Father earlier ('This is my Son . . .'). In what ways might we be tempted to doubt and question God's affirmation and love of us as his children?

- Finally, the devil explicitly invites Jesus to worship him, offering him 'all the kingdoms of the world and all their splendour' (verses 8 and 9). The thing is, they are not the devil's property to give away, but God's. In what ways might we face the subtle temptation (and real temptation is always very subtle) to pursue personal gain whilst forgetting that all good things actually belong to God anyway?
- How might Jesus' communion with his Father have grown through this experience? In what ways might we be able to grow through 'wilderness' experiences, in our relationship with God and with other people?

and there's more ...

A man found a cocoon of an Emperor moth and took it home so he could watch the moth come out of the cocoon. One day a small opening appeared. The man sat and watched the little moth for several hours as it struggled to force its body through that little hole. Then it seemed to stop making any progress. To the man it appeared as if the moth had gotten as far as it could in breaking out of the cocoon and was stuck.

Out of kindness the man decided to help the moth. He took a pair of scissors and snipped off the remaining bit of the cocoon so that the moth could get out. Soon the moth emerged, but it had a swollen body and small shrivelled wings. The man continued to watch the moth, expecting that in time the wings would enlarge and expand to be able to support the body, which would simultaneously contract to its proper size.

Neither happened. In fact, that little moth spent the rest of its life crawling around with a swollen body and shrivelled wings. It was never able to fly.

The man in his kindness and haste didn't understand that the restricting cocoon and the struggle required for the moth to get through the tiny opening were God's way of forcing fluid from the body into the wings so that the moth would be ready for flight once it achieved its freedom from the cocoon.[7]

'These things are sent to try us'. Now there's a cliché that can be uttered with too much casual ease. Do we really believe that God deliberately and purposefully sends suffering our way? Maybe not. Theology that attempts to respond to pain too simplistically sells us short of the depth and power of the gospel. But perhaps we can appreciate that there may be situations in which the experience of struggle can be the place where we discover the presence of God in unexpected ways and so learn to stay close to the one who is never as far away as we might be tempted to think.

Taking action

Notice that when Jesus faced temptation in the wilderness, he never responded to the devil by reasoned argument or discussion. Instead, his response was to cite words of Scripture. Three times he did this:

> 'One does not live by bread alone,
> but by every word that comes from the mouth of God.'
> (verse 4)

---

7. Wayne Rice (ed.), *Hot Illustrations for Youth Talks* (Grand Rapids: Zondervan, 1994), pp.85-86.

> 'Do not put the Lord your God to the test.' (verse 7)
>
> 'Worship the Lord your God,
> and serve only him.' (verse 10)

Why not try to develop this sort of habit, looking for ways of focusing on God's word in the midst of struggle and temptation? As a starter, you could try writing out by hand one, two or all three of the verses Jesus used to combat the tempter in the wilderness, and put what you have written in a place or places where it will be seen at points throughout the day – maybe beside your laptop, above the sink where you brush your teeth – even near the loo (seriously – why not?!).

Prayer

The following prayer is traditionally known as the Lorica of St Patrick:

> Christ be with me, Christ within me,
> Christ behind me, Christ before me,
> Christ beside me, Christ to win me,
> Christ to comfort and restore me,
> Christ beneath me, Christ above me,
> Christ in quiet, Christ in danger,
> Christ in hearts of all that love me,
> Christ in mouth of friend and stranger.
> Amen.[8]

---

8. Quoted in Paul Wallis, *Rough Ways in Prayer: How can I pray when I feel spiritually dead?* (London: Triangle SPCK, 1991), p. 130. Wallis' book provides an excellent discussion of what we have referred to here as the wilderness experience.

Third week of Lent
Staying close when we're feeling worried

Prayer
Lord, all of us go through times when we feel anxious and afraid. Sometimes this gets out of hand, and worrying can make us ill. Help us to understand that you want us to find freedom from this and that your word actually commands us not to worry. May we trust in you, stay close to you, and find an ever-deepening peace in you.
Amen.

Introduction
Worrying is a basic part of human experience, but when it escalates it can become very serious indeed.

Anxiety and depression are two of the most perilous yet widespread problems in our society today. Being a Christian does not immunise us from anxiety or depression (or from any other type of sickness). Faith in Jesus does not remove us from the daily challenges that everyone faces, but staying close to him empowers us to engage with and respond to those realities.

Everyone has faith of some kind. Life depends upon it. In all probability we have faith in multiple things and multiple people, but underlying all those things will be a set of core values of some description. We may not even recognise what those things are, but they are the deep things that form the foundations of the decisions we make and which tend to steer our lives. If we want to know where our faith truly lies, we need to ask exactly what that core set of values is.

Because we all have faith of some sort, it is not strictly speaking correct to talk of 'losing faith' or 'finding faith'. Rather, faith is something that is transferred from one thing into something else. We can of course find or lose our faith *in God* – but it is important to understand that if our faith is not in God, it will be in something else.

In the New Testament we find that Jesus' main teaching on the matter of anxiety brings us back to the fundamental question of where we put our faith. Staying close to him might not make the objects of our anxiety disappear, but it can enable us to see them in a rather different light.

Activity

What are you worried about right now?

Take a minute or two and write down some key words that summarise things that you are worrying about, or if you prefer, things that make you worry, even if they do not feel like live issues right now.

As we turn to the following Bible reading, instead of thinking about Jesus addressing a crowd, picture him talking to you personally, in response to the list that you have just made.

Reading: Matthew 6:24-34

'No one can serve two masters; for a slave will either hate the one and love the other, or be devoted to the one and despise the other. You cannot serve God and wealth. Therefore I tell you, do not worry about your life, what you will eat or what you will drink, or about your body, what you will wear.

Is not life more than food, and the body more than clothing? Look at the birds of the air; they neither sow nor reap nor gather into barns, and yet your heavenly Father feeds them. Are you not of more value than they? And can any of you by worrying add a single hour to your span of life? And why do you worry about clothing? Consider the lilies of the field, how they grow; they neither toil nor spin, yet I tell you, even Solomon in all his glory was not clothed like one of these. But if God so clothes the grass of the field, which is alive today and tomorrow is thrown into the oven, will he not much more clothe you – you of little faith? Therefore do not worry, saying, "What will we eat?" or "What will we drink?" or "What will we wear?" For it is the Gentiles who strive for all these things; and indeed your heavenly Father knows that you need all these things. But strive first for the kingdom of God and his righteousness, and all these things will be given to you as well.

'So do not worry about tomorrow, for tomorrow will bring worries of its own. Today's trouble is enough for today.'

Comment

Sometimes Christians think that they shouldn't suffer with anxiety or depression and that, if they do, there's something wrong with their faith. But the sort of faith that Jesus spoke of was never something that would remove our daily problems. Rather, he spoke of trusting in God our Father in such a way as to learn to see those problems differently, and so find a path to freedom. The more God becomes the focus of our thoughts and energy, the less significant other things seem, and we discover a different, liberating perspective.

In Matthew 6:24 Jesus, having talked about the meaning of true 'treasure', and the dangers of becoming preoccupied with the quest for material wealth and security, warns that 'no one can serve two masters'. In the light of such a warning, Jesus proceeds with 'therefore I tell you, do not worry about your life…'.

Discussion

- What do you think might be the link between being clear about what master we serve, and the issue of worrying?
- Jesus talks about the importance of knowing that it is God who provides for and sustains us each and every day. Two particular passages in the Old Testament make an interesting and insightful comparison. You may like to take a brief look at one or both of these:
    - *Exodus 16*. The people, led out from slavery in Egypt, find themselves wandering in the wilderness for forty years. What does this chapter of their story say about something important that God was teaching them (and us) about trusting in and relying on him?
    - *1 Kings 17:1-6* and then *7-16*. This chapter tells of two stories from the life of Elijah. In some ways they both teach us the same principle about staying close to God. What might that be?
- How do you tend to relate to other people when you're worried about something? And how do you feel about God if you're feeling stressed? How might your relationship with God and with others be impacted by a

renewed sense that God actually does have everything in hand? What do you think it would take to give you that sense of reassurance?

- One of the most unhelpful things to hear if feeling anxious or depressed can be someone else just telling us 'Don't worry; cheer up!' It can make us feel that they don't understand how we're feeling – or even that they're not really interested. But in Matthew 6:24-34 Jesus makes a very clear command: 'I tell you, do not worry.' Clearly Jesus was not saying this blithely. In what way might it be a source of strength to know that Jesus himself actually *commands* us not to worry?

and there's more...

Arturo Toscanini, the great conductor, was sitting at his podium before a concert one evening. As the orchestra warmed up just minutes before the performance, a bassoon player approached him in a fearful panic. 'Maestro, I am very sorry, but my instrument has suffered an accident, and the E-flat will not sound. I am afraid I will not be able to play tonight.'

Upon hearing this news, Toscanini went silent and closed his eyes. The bassoon player cowered in fear of his fury. The great conductor put his hands to his head and continued in silence, adding to the poor bassoon player's agony.

At last Toscanini looked up and said quietly, 'Do not worry. E-flat does not appear in your music tonight.' Toscanini had played through the entire concert in his mind, reviewing every note the bassoon player would have to play. With his intimate knowledge of the music, the conductor was able to reassure the bassoon player that everything would be all right.[9]

We may not know what lies ahead, but staying close to the one who does, and who promises to provide everything we need, enables us to see the objects of our fear and anxiety differently. A sense of the unknown may still make us feel vulnerable at times, but realising that God is with us and that he holds our future helps us to walk with a new sense of freedom.

Taking action

As a group, take a look at the following passage from Philippians 4:4-8:

> Rejoice in the Lord always; again I will say, Rejoice. Let your gentleness be known to everyone. The Lord is near. Do not worry about anything, but in everything by prayer and supplication with thanksgiving let your requests be made known to God. And the peace of God, which surpasses all understanding, will guard your hearts and your minds in Christ Jesus.
>
> Finally, beloved, whatever is true, whatever is honourable, whatever is just, whatever is pure, whatever is pleasing, whatever is commendable, if there is any excellence and if there is anything worthy of praise, think about these things.

---

9. Wayne Rice (ed.), *Hot Illustrations for Youth Talks 4* (Grand Rapids: Zondervan, 2001), p.106.

Discuss these words, then reflect on them prayerfully as one person reads them to the rest of the group. Pray together, asking for the peace of God to 'guard your hearts and your minds'.

Worrying is a universal problem – part of being human, and nobody is exempt. But for many of us it can be acute, recurrent and debilitating. If that's you, or someone you know, one book that many people have found very helpful is *The Worry Book* by Will van der Hart and Rob Waller (Nottingham: Inter-Varsity Press, 2011). More help from the same authors can be found at the online resource: www.mindandsoul.info/worry.

Prayer

Jesus,
Today I choose your peace in the face of turmoil. I choose trust in the presence of doubt. I choose courage when my will feels weak. Today I have decided to be kind to myself when it is my tendency to be critical. Today I will rest in your presence when I might try too hard. I will be a dispassionate watcher when I feel tempted to over-analyse my thoughts. Today I will be obedient to your call when I might run like Jonah. I will make light of what might have been heavy. Today I can do all this only through Christ who strengthens me. So I pray, Lord Jesus, for your strength and power in all of this and more.
For your glory,
Amen.[10]

---

10. Will van der Hart and Waller, *The Worry Book*, p.175.

Fourth week of Lent

Staying close to the glory of God

Prayer

Almighty God, by your grace you have come and made yourself known to us in Jesus. In our reflection and discussion of what it means to be close to you in a personal relationship, may we be ever mindful of your awesome holiness, and so never take that relationship casually or flippantly. May we be renewed in our reverence and respect towards you this day. Amen.

Introduction

Christian faith is not simply a matter of holding a set of beliefs. It's about relationship with God, knowing the closeness of God, and in turn, discovering how that unique relationship radically impacts the way we relate to other people. Over the last two sessions we have explored what this might mean when life hits us with the spiritual 'wilderness' or with worries. In this session, we turn our attention to the way our lives can be transformed by what might be described as 'mountaintop' experiences of God.

It is really important to understand that the glory of God is not something that can be measured by human experience. God's greatness is not calibrated by the limitations of what we have or haven't yet encountered of him. A story is told of an agnostic who travelled America lecturing on the impossibility of God. His climax to every lecture was to take out his watch and say, 'If there is a God, I defy him to strike me dead in the next five minutes.' He would stand there, waiting before his audience in silence, before walking off the stage in order to make his point. On one occasion, however, the silence was broken by one man who called out, 'Do you seriously imagine that you could exhaust the patience of almighty God in five minutes?'

==We must never reduce God to a matter of personal experience. God is far greater than that. But neither should we shy away from the important truth that God, as revealed in Jesus, is essentially relational.== The claim that God has come to us in Jesus asserts that God actually wants us to experience him. This is life-transforming, and we should expect to be taken by surprise.

Activity

If you were asked to identify the most memorable positive experience of your life (so far), what would it be? Maybe several things come to mind, but try to focus in on just one. Try to recall the occasion with as much specific detail as possible. Where were you? How old were you? What sort of time of day was it? Was anyone else with you at the time? What was so good about it and what made it so memorable? How did you feel at the time and, looking back, how do you feel when you think about it now?

Such experiences and the impression they leave on us can be life-changing. That was certainly the case for Peter, James and John in the story we are about to read ...

Reading:
Matthew 17:1-9

Six days later, Jesus took with him Peter and James and his brother John and led them up a high mountain, by themselves. And he was transfigured before them, and his face shone like the sun, and his clothes became dazzling white. Suddenly there appeared to them Moses and Elijah, talking with him. Then Peter said to Jesus, 'Lord, it is good for us to be here; if you wish, I will make three dwellings here, one for you, one for Moses, and one for Elijah.' While he was still speaking, suddenly a bright cloud overshadowed them, and from the cloud a voice said, 'This is my Son, the Beloved; with him I am well pleased; listen to him!' When the disciples heard this, they fell to the ground and were overcome by fear. But Jesus came and touched them, saying, 'Get up and do not be afraid.' And when they looked up, they saw no one except Jesus himself alone.

As they were coming down the mountain, Jesus ordered them, 'Tell no one about the vision until after the Son of Man has been raised from the dead.'

Comment

This passage is preceded by Matthew 16:21-28, in which Jesus speaks of his forthcoming suffering and death, much to the anguish and distress of Peter. However, Peter's objection is quickly rebutted by Jesus: 'If any want to become my followers, let them deny themselves and take up their cross and follow me' (verse 24). The momentary glimpse of Jesus' glory on top of the mountain is therefore set firmly in the wider context of his teaching, the focus of which has to do with the daily reality of costly discipleship in the depths of the valley. And note that as soon as they begin to make their way back down from the mountaintop and into that valley, Jesus reminds them once more that resurrection glory can only be properly understood through the lens of the cross (verse 9).

Discussion

- Have you ever had what might be described as a 'mountaintop experience' of God? What was it like? How did it change/affect you?
- What was Peter's first reaction to the transfiguration (verse 4)? Why do you think he reacted in this way? Note that it was a form of action. Being practical in our responses may be no bad thing, but in what sense might activity be a distraction?
- How do you think you would have reacted?
- How is Peter interrupted? How does this link back to what happened at Jesus' baptism (Matthew 3:13-17)?
- According to Matthew's Gospel, what happened immediately after Jesus' baptism? What might this tell us about the way in which glimpses of God's glory connect with the challenges of daily living?
- How do you think this experience may have equipped Peter, James and John for the experiences of suffering that were to come later with Jesus' death and beyond?
- What might this event teach us about the importance of seeking and staying close to the glory of God in our worship and prayer? How might such encounters empower and sustain us when life gets tough?

and there's more . . .

My wife recalls from her teenage years a family holiday which involved a day trip to a small island off the coast of West Wales. They went hoping to see some puffins. After they had walked round nearly the whole island, despondency and disappointment set in as not a single sighting had occurred. Then after several hours they eventually spotted one. Great excitement followed as they spent as much as they could afford of their remaining time on the island watching this solitary bird, photographing it and relishing the experience. Noticing that they were running out of time before the return boat to the mainland was due to leave, they made a bit of a dash around the last corner of the coastal path. Just around the bend, with only minutes to spare, they found themselves surrounded by thousands of puffins.

The reality of God's glory is far, far greater than our personal experience of it. Every now and then we may be privileged to encounter something, albeit a glimpse, of the sheer wonder and greatness of God. Peter, James and John were blessed with this. But even for them, the experience was just a tiny snapshot of an immeasurably greater reality.

Encounters with the living God are life-transforming. They empower us in the face of the challenges of daily life in the 'valley', whatever that may be for each of us. But we should always be mindful that our own experience, however powerful, is very limited. Next time you find yourself feeling like you're on top of the mountain, remember that this is nothing compared with what's in store for all eternity!

Taking action

Most of our lives are not 'on top of the mountain' but 'in the valley' of ordinary, daily life. Reflect as a group on what 'the valley' means to you, and then take this before God in prayer, asking him to inspire and equip you accordingly.

Prayer
Living God,
we praise you for your sovereign power
through which you have transformed our lives,
bringing strength, joy, hope and peace.
We thank you for the power that flows within us through Christ
and the living presence of the Holy Spirit,
equipping us to see life in a new way
and to meet each day with confidence.
Yet we are conscious that you want your life-changing power
to flow through us,
reaching out into the world beyond.
Forgive us that we have failed to let that happen,
so concerned with self
that we have forgotten our responsibility to others.
Forgive the narrowness of our vision that has led us
to store up rather than be conduits of
your renewing grace.
Move within us,
and open our lives to all that you are able to do,
so that in your name we may live and work for you,
through Jesus Christ our Lord.
Amen.[11]

---

11. Nick Fawcett, *2000 Prayers for Public Worship* (Stowmarket: Kevin Mayhew, 2008), #1574.

Fifth week of Lent
Staying close in our witness

Prayer

Loving God, you reach out to us in Jesus. In him you choose to make yourself vulnerable, entering our world of pain and suffering, even to the point of death on the cross. As we think about what it means to be witnesses to these things, grant us the courage to embrace vulnerability and to reach out to others, that they too may know your love.
Amen.

Introduction

Several years ago my family and I were walking on Dartmoor. Our children were very young and it was a bit of a struggle getting them to climb the hill to the tor that we were aiming for, but eventually we did it. At about halfway up we noticed the figure of a man standing on top of the tor. He was waving frantically. Before we could reach him, he had already climbed down and was running towards us. As he approached, somewhat out of breath, he told us very excitedly that this had been the first time that he had ventured outside on his own for about two years. He went on to explain that in the past he had been an active rock climber, until one day he suffered a very nasty accident. Narrowly escaping death, he was told he might never walk properly again, let alone climb. However, it seemed that he had defied all the odds, because after several operations and a very long, gradual process of physiotherapy, he had made a remarkable recovery. As he shared his story with us, tears of joy welled up in his eyes. My wife and I were speechless. 'I'm so sorry,' he said, 'I'm just so happy, I had to tell someone, and you're the only ones here.'

Before we had managed to process what we had heard and respond, the man was on his way.

What a privilege it was to have been on the receiving end of this man's overwhelming joy. Most of all, it reminded us that when something amazing happens to you, you just have to tell others. British reserve gives way to something deeper – the barriers go down as we cannot contain that which just has to be shared. We must tell the world. It would seem unnatural not to want to.

As Christians we are called to witness to others of the things that God has done and is doing in our lives (Acts 1:8). That may sound scary at times, because it can send us to places where we feel vulnerable. But perhaps there are occasions when we shy away simply because we have misunderstood what 'witnessing' actually means. If we think that talking about our faith might sound forced and contrived, then maybe we have a misguided image in our minds as to what it means to tell others about Jesus. A different view is possible though. It is the most natural thing in the world to want to share good things with others, whether it is music, food, stories – indeed anything that has made a positive difference to our own lives. And it's not really different when it comes to sharing our faith.

The presence of God's Spirit in our lives is the very reality that we are called to be witnesses of. Seeking and staying close to this reality is vital therefore not only to our own discipleship, but for the sake of others too.

Activity

Think of a time when you had some news that you were bursting to share with someone else. What was it? Perhaps it was an engagement, the birth of a child, the passing of an exam or getting a job. Whatever it was, try to recall the details of that time – where you were, who it was that you were itching to tell (it may have been everyone!) and, most significantly, what it felt like to be carrying such a burden of good news.

In Matthew 5, Jesus gives us two images which convey how authentic Christian witness is something very natural indeed. We are called to be *sprinkled* and to *shine*...

Reading:
Matthew 5:13-16

'You are the salt of the earth; but if salt has lost its taste, how can its saltiness be restored? It is no longer good for anything, but is thrown out and trampled under foot.

You are the light of the world. A city built on a hill cannot be hidden. No one after lighting a lamp puts it under the bushel basket, but on the lampstand, and it gives light to all in the house. In the same way, let your light shine before others, so that they may see your good works and give glory to your Father in heaven.'

Comment

Christian witness involves our words and our actions but, as with every aspect of our discipleship, it is more concerned with our 'being' than with our 'doing'. That is to say, the things we say and do are important, but to be authentic they need to be grounded in knowing who we are in Christ. Notice then that Jesus uses the images of salt and light to describe our *identity* ('you *are* the salt of the earth; you *are* the light of the world'). Words and deeds that really do point to the reality of God are born out of knowing and staying close to that reality.

Discussion

- An old saying goes, 'we are called to be witnesses, not judges'. What are the key differences between a witness and a judge? In what ways might we distort our Christian witness by acting as judges?

- Reflect on the image of 'salt' and 'saltiness'. Today we tend to associate salt predominantly with flavouring, but in the ancient world it would have been chiefly used for preserving – that is, keeping things fresh. It would also have been used for cleansing and disinfecting. Considering these images, what might it mean for us to be the 'salt of the earth'?

- Now spend some time thinking about the image of 'light'. What might it mean to be the 'light of the world'?

- What *does* happen if you light a lamp and put it under a bowl (verse 15)? What is Jesus saying to us when he gives us this image? What does it mean to 'let our light shine'? How might this be challenging, even scary?

- A lamp on a stand gives out light but is also exposed and vulnerable. In what sort of practical ways might witnessing to God's love make us feel exposed and vulnerable?

- For salt to be used it needs to be sprinkled. This means that the grains are taken out of the pot and scattered. It may be relatively easy to talk openly about our faith when we are gathered with other Christians (for example at church meetings on Sundays). In what ways might we be called to be a 'sprinkled' and 'scattered' presence throughout the week? In what sorts of situation might we find ourselves to be the only Christian believer present? How can we make a difference in those contexts?
- How might allowing ourselves to become vulnerable for God draw us closer to him?

and there's more...

Imagine that you happen to sit down in front of the television one day and find there is a cookery show on. Maybe it's not the sort of thing that you normally watch, but on this occasion there's something about the particular dish being prepared that catches your attention. You find yourself watching for several minutes until you decide to look up the recipe on the website mentioned by the TV presenter. The recipe looks straightforward enough, and you resolve to attempt the dish some time in the not-too-distant future.

Several days later you are thinking about what to cook for dinner. You remember the recipe that you downloaded and notice that you have all the ingredients already in the kitchen. This particular recipe is different from anything you have ever tried before, and as you cook, you are surprised by the simplicity with which it all comes together.

Eventually the food is ready. You begin to eat. It tastes wonderful. You have never before experienced such a combination of herbs and spices and you quickly conclude that this is the most delicious thing you have ever tasted.

Your enthusiasm for the dish becomes so great that you phone a group of friends and invite them over to dinner the following weekend. You don't usually organise dinner parties, but you are so keen to share this culinary discovery that you find you have issued the invitations before you have really had time to think long and hard about it. And everyone you have invited is coming.

Then, on the morning of the day that you are due to cook for your friends, you suddenly begin to panic. It dawns on you that you are not used to cooking for others, and you start to worry about all the things that could go wrong. What if they don't like the food? What if they start to ask you lots of technical questions about the ingredients which you are unable to answer? As you mull these things over, you begin to get cold feet, concerned that you may make a fool of yourself. Wondering whether you should call the whole thing off, you remember again the succulence of the food and the simplicity of its preparation. Staying close to that thought, you carry on with your plans.

Later on that night, as you share the meal with your friends, you wonder what all the worry was about.

When all is said and done, 'Christian witness' really is about sharing, and it's as simple as that. It may make us feel a little nervous, for all sorts of reasons. But God calls us to leave our personal insecurities behind and stay close to his goodness.

Taking action

Letting our light shine, and being open to spending time in those places that God chooses to 'sprinkle' and 'scatter' us involves a willingness to embrace vulnerability. We each have our own comfort zones. Ask yourself what yours are. Then ask God to show you what it might mean for you to step out of those. Really pray about this, asking God to give you one or two practical opportunities to step out in faith and reach out to someone else in a way that you haven't done before. It may involve making a phone call, instigating a conversation, going to visit someone or undertaking something that is quite alien to your own experience (so far). Pray for God's courage. Then do it.

Prayer

Make me a channel of your peace.
Where there is hatred let me bring your love;
Where there is injury, your pardon, Lord;
And where there's doubt, true faith in you:

Oh, Master, grant that I may never seek
So much to be consoled as to console;
To be understood as to understand;
To be loved, as to love with all my soul.

Make me a channel of your peace.
Where there's despair in life, let me bring hope;
Where there is darkness, only light;
And where there's sadness, ever joy:

Make me a channel of your peace.
It is in pardoning that we are pardoned,
In giving of ourselves that we receive,
And in dying that we're born to eternal life.
Amen.[12]

---

12. The words of this hymn by Sebastian Temple are based on what is traditionally known as the Prayer of St Francis, although the attribution to St Francis of Assisi is erroneous. ©OCP Publications, 1967.

Sixth week of Lent
Staying close to the servant king

Prayer

Almighty God, creator and sustainer of the universe, you are the Lord of lords and the King of kings. Yet you come to us in Jesus as the one who serves – washing feet, embracing the outcast and entering suffering and death in order to set us free for life in all its fullness. As we reflect on what you have done for us, may we be led into a deeper understanding of what we can do for you and your kingdom.
Amen.

Introduction

A term often used to denote the Christian virtue of humility is 'servant-hearted'. It helpfully expresses what is described in Philippians 2:5-8 as Christ's own attitude, which his followers are called to reflect:

> Let the same mind be in you that was in Christ Jesus,
> who, though he was in the form of God,
>   did not regard equality with God
>   as something to be exploited,
> but emptied himself,
>   taking the form of a slave,
>   being born in human likeness.
> And being found in human form,
>   he humbled himself
>   and became obedient to the point of death –
>   even death on a cross.

To say that a person is 'servant-hearted' could potentially be misleading though. This is because it implies that some people have a heart that is readily disposed to be of service, whereas others do not. The truth is every human heart has a certain proclivity to serve something or someone. It may not be consciously recognised, but we are all servants of one kind or another. Maybe our service is to ourselves, driven towards financial gain, or to achieve power. Our service might be given over to a vision of what we want our life to look like in terms of career, family, and what we consider to be security. It might be that we do serve others, but deep down inside, such service is motivated by a sense of guilt over something, or a lack of self-worth, or simply a longing to be liked.

If we are serious about getting close and staying close to the servant-heart we see in Jesus, we need to begin by facing up to the reality that the problem is not *whether* we serve, but *who* or *what* we serve. And no matter how hard and how subtly we may try to convince ourselves otherwise, we can never be the servant of more than one master.

Activity

Looking back on your recent experience (say, in the last few days or couple of weeks), try to think of as many different ways in which you may have served other people. In each case, ask yourself:

What sort of service was it?

Was it a 'large' or 'small' act of service?

What cost was it to you to engage in this act of service? Did you do it because it was part of your job (that is, you were paid to do it)? If not, was it something you did as part of a structured voluntary 'role' (for example, serving refreshments because it was your turn on the rota), or was it more spontaneous?

Ask yourself the question: what were your motivations for choosing to serve (chances are they vary from task to task)? What does it feel like when you serve in these various ways?

In the passage that follows we see how people gave great honour to Jesus. As we read these words, we need to remember that the event was the prelude to the greatest act of servanthood that history has ever known . . .

Reading:
Matthew 21:1-11

When they had come near Jerusalem and had reached Bethphage, at the Mount of Olives, Jesus sent two disciples, saying to them, 'Go into the village ahead of you, and immediately you will find a donkey tied, and a colt with her; untie them and bring them to me. If anyone says anything to you, just say this, "The Lord needs them." And he will send them immediately.' This took place to fulfil what had been spoken through the prophet, saying,

> 'Tell the daughter of Zion,
> Look, your king is coming to you,
> humble, and mounted on a donkey,
> and on a colt, the foal of a donkey.'

The disciples went and did as Jesus had directed them; they brought the donkey and the colt, and put their cloaks on them, and he sat on them. A very large crowd spread their cloaks on the road, and others cut branches from the trees and spread them on the road. The crowds that went ahead of him and that followed were shouting,

> 'Hosanna to the Son of David!
> Blessed is the one who comes in the name of the Lord!
> Hosanna in the highest heaven!'

When he entered Jerusalem, the whole city was in turmoil, asking, 'Who is this?' The crowds were saying, 'This is the prophet Jesus from Nazareth in Galilee.'

Comment

As the story unfolds, there is a growing sense that Jesus knows what lies ahead (verses 2 and 3). Luke 9:51 tells us that Jesus 'set his face' to go to Jerusalem. The cross does not deter him. The very opposite. Jesus' resolve is manifest at those very points where he predicts his own suffering and death (Matthew 16:21-28; 20:17).

As crowds gather, extolling Jesus with 'Hosanna', he knows that in only a few days the very same voices will be shouting, 'Crucify him!'. And still he advances, readily embracing whatever it takes to bring salvation to those who will betray him, deny him, flee from him, inflict pain on him and kill him. His motivation is simply to do the will of his Father (Matthew 26:39), deep in the knowledge that he has come 'not to be served but to serve' (Matthew 20:28). Jesus shows us that true servanthood is not about self-debasement for its own sake – but a heart that yearns for the Father's will to be done. An authentically Christian servant-heart is one that is not caught up with itself but focuses on God. It's about being self-forgetful. As Rick

Warren puts it, humility is 'not thinking less of ourselves, but thinking of ourselves *less*'.[13]

Discussion

- It's easy for us to agree on the principle of serving others as a key aspect of Christian discipleship. But what sort of things can make it very difficult in practice?
- How does the image of Christ as servant inspire you to serve others?
- Verse 8 tells us that a very large crowd spread their cloaks on the road, as an expression of honour and respect to Jesus. To these people their cloaks may have been one of their most valuable belongings. Think about what the image of the 'cloak' might represent to you. What things are really important to you? What, in practical terms, might it mean to lay those things down in service to Jesus?
- Many who shouted 'hosanna' at the beginning of the week shouted 'crucify him' at the end of it. Can you think of any ways in which similar contradictions might be found in our own lives today?
- Verse 10 tells us that 'the whole city was stirred and asked "who is this?"'. How and why might people today be intrigued by the notion that, in Jesus, God comes to us not to be served but to serve?

---

13. Rick Warren, *The Purpose Driven Life* (Grand Rapids: Zondervan, 2002), p.265.

and there's more...

Rick Warren writes:

> If you are not involved in any service or ministry, what excuse have you been using? Abraham was old, Jacob was insecure, Leah was unattractive, Joseph was abused, Moses stuttered, Gideon was poor, Samson was co-dependent, Rahab was immoral, David had an affair and all kinds of family problems, Elijah was suicidal, Jeremiah was depressed, Jonah was reluctant, Naomi was a widow, John the Baptist was eccentric to say the least, Peter was impulsive and hot-tempered, Martha worried a lot, the Samaritan woman had several failed marriages, Zacchaeus was unpopular, Thomas had doubts, Paul had poor health, and Timothy was timid. That's quite a variety of misfits, but God used each of them in his service. He will use you, too, if you stop making excuses.[14]

If we focus on our own human faults and weaknesses (which can be a combination of perceived and actual realities), it's not hard to persuade ourselves that we haven't much to offer in service. And so we hold back. But service itself is not actually difficult. Anyone and everyone can serve in some way or another. Often what is needed is to recognise that God sees us differently than we see ourselves, and then to refocus on his grace and power that can enable amazing things to happen when we are willing to entrust him with who we are and what we have. Staying close to his grace and power is vital.

---

14. Quoted in Mark Stibbe, *A Basket of Gems* (Oxford: Monarch, 2009), p.145.

Taking action

Staying close in our prayer life, our worship and our meditation to the image of the Christ who serves can make a real difference in shaping us into Christ-like people.

As a group, take a look at or listen to the words of Graham Kendrick's song 'The Servant King (From Heaven you came)'.[15] Take time to reflect on each line in turn. Don't rush this. Then, in prayer, ask God to show you one way in which you might serve him through serving others. It might be that God confirms in your heart that you are already doing the very thing that he wants you to do. It's also possible that there may be something new in store...

Prayer

Almighty God,
whose most dear Son went not up to joy
but first he suffered pain,
and entered not into glory before he was crucified:
mercifully grant that we, walking in the way of the cross,
may find it to be the way of life and peace;
through Jesus Christ our Lord.
Amen.[16]

---

15. © Thankyou Music, 1983 (see http://grahamkendrick.co.uk/songs/item/23-the-servant-king-from-heaven-you-came)
16. Closing prayer from the service for Good Friday, Trustees for Methodist Church Purposes, *The Methodist Service Book* (Peterborough: Methodist Publishing House, 1999), p.264.

Easter

Staying close to the risen Jesus

Prayer
Lord, in the chaos of their grief and despair, you took your first followers by surprise by showing them that you are far closer than they had realised. Help us, like them, to be shaken and stirred by your resurrection power, that we may see life and death differently. May we too be transformed by the life-giving power of your Spirit, and may we stay close to that reality every day.
Amen.

Introduction
One of my favourite television series of all time is *Inspector Morse*, closely followed by its sequel, *Lewis*. I could watch the same episodes over and over again (in fact, I do) and still not get bored. Why? Because I love the characters, the drama and the story. But for all my enjoyment of watching repeats of these programmes, the experience is never quite as special as seeing them for the first time.

The power of a really great story will be such that we are gripped by it even though we know what happens in the end. But such stories are never quite so powerful as the first time we hear them, for it is then that we really enter into the story and are engaged by the suspense of not knowing how things will turn out.

When we read the Gospels, we must beware of our familiarity with them. We know that Jesus did not stay in the grave – that out of his death came resurrection. But the first disciples didn't.

To rediscover the power of the Easter story, we need to approach it not as a story whose ending we already know, but as though we were watching it unfold for the first time. Only then can we be brought close to the experience of the earliest followers of Jesus for whom, more than for anyone else in history, reality was turned completely upside down.

Activity

Think of a time when you were taken by surprise in a really positive, pleasing and encouraging way. Maybe you were on the receiving end of a completely unexpected act of radical kindness. Perhaps you were reunited with a long-lost friend in an unexpected way. It may have been that someone said something to you which you simply didn't see coming, but which transformed your day.

How did the experience make you feel? Spend some time reflecting on this. The women in the story that follows had the greatest surprise the world has ever known . . .

Reading:
Matthew 28:1-10

After the sabbath, as the first day of the week was dawning, Mary Magdalene and the other Mary went to see the tomb. And suddenly there was a great earthquake; for an angel of the Lord, descending from heaven, came and rolled back the stone and sat on it. His appearance was like lightning, and his clothing white as snow. For fear of him the guards shook and became like dead men. But the angel said to the women, 'Do not be afraid; I know that you are looking for Jesus who was crucified. He is not here; for he has been raised, as he said. Come, see the place where he lay. Then go quickly and tell his disciples, "He has been raised from the dead, and indeed he is going ahead of you to Galilee; there you will see him." This is my message for you.' So they left the tomb quickly with fear and great joy, and ran to tell his disciples. Suddenly Jesus met them and said, 'Greetings!' And they came to him, took hold of his feet, and worshipped him. Then Jesus said to them, 'Do not be afraid; go and tell my brothers to go to Galilee; there they will see me.'

Comment

Matthew's account of the women at the tomb really drives home the theme that, in Christ, the extraordinary bursts right in on the ordinary. The events leading up to the crucifixion of Jesus, and his death itself, were not of course 'ordinary'. But the women's experience of grief, shock and bewilderment as they mourn the sudden death of the one they loved, and with it, the dashing of their deepest hopes, is something that all of us can connect with at some time or another in various ways and at different levels. For them, further drama is added to what is already a major crisis. Having come to visit the tomb in order to express that which is on their hearts and which holds them in a state of confusion and dismay, there is no opportunity to pause for quiet reflection and to simply sob away some of the pain. Earthquake! Lightning! An angel appears! It's all too much for the Roman guards, but the women remain conscious enough to hear the angelic message. Fear fuses with joy as they run, but they don't get very far before meeting with the risen one himself, who simply greets them. This is the one whose extraordinary peace and power we need to draw near to, and stay close to, in the midst of the ordinariness of our daily lives.

Discussion

- Jesus' resurrection is at the very heart of authentic Christian faith (see 1 Corinthians 15). This may seem obvious, but why is it so central?
- How do you think you would have reacted if you were one of the first ones to come face to face with the risen Jesus? How do you think you would feel? What would you say or do?
- Winston Churchill apparently once said something like this: 'Every now and then humans stumble upon the truth. The trouble is, most of the time they pick themselves up and walk on as though nothing had ever happened.' To what extent might we have become 'too familiar' with the resurrection story, to the extent that we fail to grasp the depth and power of its truth in our daily lives?
- This course has been all about the importance of 'staying close' to God in Christ. Verse 9, above, says that the women 'took hold of his feet'. In their culture such an act represented an expression of homage and submission reserved for kings and rulers. What might it mean for us to do this in worship, prayer and contemplation?
- In an average day, the chances are that each of us is preoccupied with something. It may be something very mundane; it may be something that causes us to feel anxious. How might it make a difference if we strove to make the risen Jesus the object of our preoccupation?
- In what practical ways might we do this?

and there's more . . .

One October afternoon in 1982, an American football game was being played in a stadium in Madison, Wisconsin. More than 60,000 Wisconsin fans had turned out to support their team. Before long it became clear that they were not going to win. Strangely though, the more the score stacked up against their team, the louder the Wisconsin fans cheered. They were suffering an all-out defeat, yet the supporters seemed to be full of joy as though they were cruising their way towards victory. What was happening?

It transpired that seventy miles away Wisconsin's baseball team, the Milwaukee Brewers, were winning Game Three of the 1982 World Series. Back in the stands of the football stadium in Madison, many of the Wisconsin fans had portable radios, and were listening to their baseball triumph. While on the field before them was defeat, their attention was on a victory that they could not see but knew was real.[17]

All around and about us things may seem to be falling apart. The world in which we live is broken and chaotic. But we are called to tune into and stay close to a different reality – the risen Jesus.

Taking action

Spend some time as a group in prayer, maybe with some background music, or just in silence, reflecting on the fact

---

17. Paraphrased from Wayne Rice (ed.), *More Hot Illustrations for Youth Talks* (Grand Rapids: Zondervan, 1995), p.148.

that Jesus is indeed alive and is with us through his Spirit. Ponder the notion that he is closer to you even than your own breath. Don't hurry this – take your time, asking Jesus to touch you in a new and different way and allow him the opportunity to do so.

Following on from this – and here's where it perhaps becomes more of a challenge – try to think of one or two ways in which you may be reminded of God's closeness in the midst of your daily life in future.

Here are some suggestions:

- Set an alarm, maybe on your watch, phone or tablet, to remind you in the middle of each day to pause, maybe only for a few seconds, but long enough to put the brakes on and revisit the truth that God is close to you. You could do this at 12 noon exactly, or maybe some other time that works better for you.

- Put a note or maybe a symbolic object such as a small wooden cross near the place where you brush your teeth. Every time you do so, it will remind you to think for a moment about the presence of the risen Jesus.

- The same sort of thing could be done by the kitchen sink, so that washing-up could become a time to re-tune your awareness of God's presence in the midst of the mundane.

- Select an image as the desktop or screen saver on your computer which will remind you that God is close. You might choose some words of scripture or something like a picture of an empty tomb. Whatever you decide, it may be helpful to change it every so often, so that it doesn't lose any impact on you.

There are endless things you could do. Be creative. This isn't about 'religious duty', but about taking one or two steps to help you remember that God is far closer to you than you probably recognise.

Prayer
Living God,
we praise you for the wonder of Easter –
this day that changed the world forever!
We rejoice in the victory of Christ:
his triumph over evil,
hatred,
despair,
and even death itself.
Living God,
we praise you for the victory you have won,
and for the assurance it brings that nothing in life or death
can ever separate us from your love;
nothing in heaven or earth defeat your loving purpose for all the world.
To you be praise and glory,
this day and always.
Amen.[18]

---

18. Nick Fawcett, *2000 Prayers for Public Worship*, #256.

Postscript
Something for the journey

In the Christian calendar we often refer to various 'seasons', such as Advent, Lent, and of course, Easter. I've always found it slightly amusing that in various liturgical resources the periods in between such seasons are referred to as 'ordinary' time. If Jesus really is alive, there is no more going back to the 'ordinary' for us – or rather, 'ordinary' is given a whole new meaning. Easter cannot be regarded as a passing season. Of course seasons come and go – the experience of change and transition remains part of what it is to be human. But the gospel urges and reassures us that we can now lay hold of a new identity, *in Christ*, as a *new creation* (2 Corinthians 5:17). God has drawn close to us in Jesus, intimately so, and God calls us to know that.

Take a look at these words from Luke's Gospel:

Reading:
Luke 24:13-32

Now on that same day two of them were going to a village called Emmaus, about seven miles from Jerusalem, and talking with each other about all these things that had happened. While they were talking and discussing, Jesus himself came near and went with them, but their eyes were kept from recognizing him. And he said to them, 'What are you discussing with each other while you walk along?' They stood still, looking sad. Then one of them, whose name was

Cleopas, answered him, 'Are you the only stranger in Jerusalem who does not know the things that have taken place there in these days?' He asked them, 'What things?' They replied, 'The things about Jesus of Nazareth, who was a prophet mighty in deed and word before God and all the people, and how our chief priests and leaders handed him over to be condemned to death and crucified him. But we had hoped that he was the one to redeem Israel. Yes, and besides all this, it is now the third day since these things took place. Moreover, some women of our group astounded us. They were at the tomb early this morning, and when they did not find his body there, they came back and told us that they had indeed seen a vision of angels who said that he was alive. Some of those who were with us went to the tomb and found it just as the women had said; but they did not see him.' Then he said to them, 'Oh, how foolish you are, and how slow of heart to believe all that the prophets have declared! Was it not necessary that the Messiah should suffer these things and then enter into his glory?' Then beginning with Moses and all the prophets, he interpreted to them the things about himself in all the scriptures.

As they came near the village to which they were going, he walked ahead as if he were going on. But they urged him strongly, saying, 'Stay with us, because it is almost evening and the day is now nearly over.' So he went in to stay with them. When he was at the table with them, he took bread, blessed and broke it, and gave it to them. Then their eyes were opened, and they recognized him; and he vanished from their sight. They said to each other, 'Were not our hearts burning within us while he was talking to us on the road, while he was opening the scriptures to us?'

Staying close

They weren't aware of it, but the risen Jesus was journeying right beside these disenchanted disciples as they walked along. Eventually came the moment of realisation – he had been close to them all the while, and they had just not realised it.

As this course of study and reflection draws to a close, the story of the road to Emmaus leaves us with a simple yet profoundly important truth that we would do well to finish with – or rather, start with – as we journey on:

> Whatever life might be throwing at us right now, God is much closer than we recognise.

We may not always *feel* God's presence, but scripture tells us that he is much, much closer than we think. Remember that. Dwell on it, contemplate, meditate and pray over it. Let it become your preoccupation such that it shapes and defines the way you think, live, and talk.

Stay close.

Prayer

Lord, thank you that you are closer to us than our own breath. Forgive us for when we live as though you weren't there at all. Help us to remember that in every season of our lives you are intimately close to us in your resurrection power – even when we are not aware of it. Just as you draw near to us in Jesus, help us to draw near to you and to stay close to you, every day.
Amen.